The Scorpion King

MAX ALLAN COLLINS

Based on a motion picture screenplay by
STEPHEN SOMMERS and
WILL OSBORNE and
DAVID HAYTER
Story by JONATHAN HALES and
STEPHEN SOMMERS

Level 2

Retold by Andy Hopkins and Jocelyn Potter
Series Editors: Andy Hopkins and Jocelyn Potter

Pearson Education Limited
Edinburgh Gate, Harlow,
Essex CM20 2JE, England
and Associated Companies throughout the world.

ISBN 0582 779715

First published by Berkley Boulevard 2002
This edition published by Penguin Books 2003

3 5 7 9 10 8 6 4 2

Typeset by Ferdinand Pageworks, Surrey
Set in 11/14pt Bembo
Printed in China
SWTC/03

Published by Pearson Education Limited in association with
Penguin Books Ltd, both companies being subsidiaries of Pearson Plc

For a complete list of the titles available in the Penguin Readers series please write to your local
Pearson Education office or to: Penguin Readers Marketing Department,
Pearson Education, Edinburgh Gate, Harlow, Essex CM20 2JE.

Contents

Introduction

The Teacher of Men looked at Mathayus.

"An Akkadian," he said. "This is nice." He smiled, but it wasn't a friendly smile. "Akkadians are never afraid. Am I right? Let's see."

He hit Mathayus hard across his face.

Most Akkadians are dead now. Memnon, the "Teacher of Men," is winning every fight. He is taking countries and killing everybody in them. He wants the world. He wants to be the Scorpion King.

Can Mathayus stop him? First, he has to kill Memnon's sorcerer. The sorcerer can see the future and helps Memnon with his plans. But sorcerers don't die easily . . .

The Scorpion King is an exciting story of love and hate. There are good men and bad men, strong men and weak men—and very strong women. Some people live, but many people have to die. In these difficult times, who are your friends? How can Mathayus know? And can he change his future?

Max Allan Collins wrote the book of *The Scorpion King* from the story of the movie by Jonathan Hales, Stephen Sommers, David Hayter, and Will Osborne. In the movie, Stephen Brand is Memnon, Kelly Hu is Cassandra, and The Rock is Mathayus. The Rock also played the Scorpion King in the movie of *The Mummy Returns*. *The Mummy* and *The Mummy Returns* are Penguin Readers too.

Chapter 1   "Somebody is watching me."

Inside their mountain palace, Memnon's fighters ate and drank. They told stories and they fought. They were bad men—but everything around them, from the cold mountains to the hot desert, was Memnon's country now.

A cold, bored guard stood outside the building. He wanted to be inside with his friends. He died quickly, before he knew it. He fell into the snow.

Another guard heard something. What was that? A hand took his leg and pulled him down. In minutes he was dead.

The killer was Mathayus, an Akkadian man with very dark eyes. He was a fighter too, but he was a good man. He was there because Jesup, another Akkadian, was a prisoner inside the building.

Mathayus killed two more guards. Then he climbed slowly up the outside wall. He took a large rock with him. He moved quickly to the chimney and climbed down into it with the rock above his head. When the rock was in the top of the chimney, no smoke from the fire inside could leave the room.

Now the room was full of thick, black smoke. The fighters turned to the fire, but they couldn't see Mathayus. He killed five men before he walked out of the smoke. His face was black, but his eyes and his smile were white. The other fighters ran to the door.

The prisoner, Jesup, looked up from the floor.

"Kill them!" he said. "I told them, 'My brother will kill *all* of you.'"

Mathayus laughed and helped his brother up on his feet. Then they went outside and found their horses. Suddenly, Mathayus stopped and looked up.

"What is it?" Jesup asked.

"I don't know. I feel that somebody is watching me."

And yes, in another place, in the city of Gomorrah, a sorcerer watched Mathayus, the Akkadian fighter.

The sorcerer watched and waited.

Chapter 2   "The sorcerer will die."

Memnon's name meant "Teacher of Men," but his lessons were hard. He took prisoners and killed them. He took women and used them. When his fighters came, most people ran from them. Some men stayed and fought for their homes. They died.

There was only one small country of free men and women, and the name of the place was Ur. People from other countries came to Ur too because they had no homes now.

The people of Ur and their visitors stood around a fire in front of King Pheron and his son, Takmet.

"We are here," King Pheron said, "because we have to fight Memnon."

A Nubian woman stood up. She was tall, dark, and very beautiful. Around her were her fighters—also beautiful women.

"Those are fine words, Pheron," Isis said. "But Memnon has thousands of fighters—and he has his sorcerer. The sorcerer sees everything and he knows everything. With his help, Memnon cannot lose."

"Then we will kill the sorcerer," King Pheron answered.

"You are crazy! We cannot fight Memnon!" Balthazar was a Nubian too. He was a large man, the size of a mountain. "I am not going to watch my men die."

"*Your* men, Balthazar? You are not a king," Takmet said.

"I am their king, little man."

Takmet laughed at him. "You are king of nothing—only sand and rocks."

Balthazar was a large man, the size of a mountain.

Balthazar moved quickly and pushed the young man to the ground. He pulled out his sword and the king's guards jumped up. Then a knife flew over Balthazar's sword and into a tree.

Everybody looked around. It was Mathayus.

"Memnon can sit and wait for this country," he said. "You will all die before he has to kill you!"

He walked to the front with two friends.

"Akkadians!" Balthazar said. "Aren't they all dead?"

"These are the last Akkadians," King Pheron said. "And they will kill Memnon's sorcerer."

"These people don't kill for their country or their people," Balthazar said. "They kill for money."

Mathayus looked at him, but said nothing.

"And how much will these killers cost?" Takmet asked his father.

"Twenty red rubies," King Pheron said quietly.

"Father!" Takmet shouted. "That's all of our money!"

"Be quiet, boy!"

Takmet walked angrily away.

King Pheron looked at the people in front of him.

"When the sorcerer is dead, will you fight with me?" he asked.

They thought about this. Then, slowly, they said yes. Only Balthazar, the Nubian, said nothing. Everybody waited. Then he too said yes.

King Pheron gave the bag of rubies to Jesup, the oldest of the Akkadians.

"The sorcerer will die," Jesup said, and the three men began to leave.

"Killer!" Balthazar called behind them.

Mathayus turned quickly and Balthazar threw his knife back at him.

The Akkadian caught it easily. Then he looked at King Pheron.

Mathayus looked at Balthazar, but said nothing.

"When you want us to kill *him*," he told the king, "you will not have to pay us."

The three Akkadians walked away from the fire, into the night.

Chapter 3   "I am Cassandra."

The Akkadians rode across the desert. Jesup and Rama were on horses. Mathayus was on his dirty white camel, Hanna.

At the end of the day they found the tents of Memnon's fighters. They killed the first two guards quickly and quietly. Then they went different ways.

Mathayus killed two more men before he found his brother and his friend again. They looked around and their eyes fell on one tent. It was different—larger than the other tents, with strange pictures on the outside. The home of a sorcerer ...

They moved quietly to the tent with their knives in their hands. Then the bottom of the tent moved and showed them the feet of guards inside it—a lot of guards. Did Memnon know about the Akkadians?

"Let's go back," Mathayus said.

But the door of the tent opened and arrows shot out. More arrows came from a tent behind them. Mathayus jumped up above the arrows, onto the top of the large tent, but the arrows hit the other two Akkadians.

Mathayus looked down unhappily. He couldn't help them. He cut the top of the tent and jumped down inside it.

And there was the sorcerer. The sorcerer was a beautiful woman! He had to shoot her—but he couldn't. Why couldn't he do it?

"I am Cassandra," she said, but her mouth didn't move. The sound was inside his head. "They betrayed you, Mathayus."

The sorcerer was a beautiful woman!

"You know my name?" he said.

"Yes. I also know that you want to kill me. You can try."

Mathayus felt weak. He couldn't shoot.

Suddenly, a guard ran into the tent. Mathayus killed him. Then he took out another arrow.

"I am sorry, Akkadian," Cassandra said. She sounded sad.

Another guard ran in. Mathayus took out his sword and killed him too. Then there were more guards. He killed three and fought the other men. But he couldn't kill all of them.

Memnon came in and stood in front of him. And, in his head, Mathayus heard Cassandra say again, "I am sorry, Akkadian. I am sorry."

Chapter 4   "Akkadians do not die easily."

The Teacher of Men looked at Mathayus.

"An Akkadian," he said. "This is nice." He smiled, but it wasn't a friendly smile. "Akkadians are never afraid. Am I right? Let's see."

He hit Mathayus hard across his face.

"No fine words now?" A man in the doorway spoke—Takmet, the son of King Pheron of Ur!

"You, Takmet?" Mathayus said. "You are our betrayer? You are betraying your *father*?"

The king's son smiled.

"My father did not listen to me," he said. "He paid for his mistake."

Takmet put his hand into his bag and took out his father's head.

The guards looked at it. Cassandra turned away. Only Memnon laughed.

"Takmet," he said, "you can fight with me now. When we take Ur, you can go back there."

The door to the tent opened and two guards arrived with a

prisoner. Jesup! He was almost dead, but he turned his head. He looked at Mathayus.

"Another Akkadian!" Memnon said. "Akkadians do not die easily! Bring him to me."

He killed Jesup.

Mathyus could do nothing. Cassandra closed her eyes, then opened them again.

Memnon looked at his knife.

"It is a good knife," he said. "I think I will use it again now."

He looked at Mathayus.

"Stop! Wait!" Cassandra said. "I know the future and Mathayus will not die today. You and your men cannot kill him—or you will die too."

Memnon thought about this. Then Thorak, one of his fighters, hit Mathayus hard.

♦

"It is a good knife," Memnon said.

When Mathayus woke up, the sun was high. All around him were rocks and sand. He was under the sand—only his head was above it. He couldn't move.

Guards watched him from a rock. Next to him was the head of another prisoner.

"I'm here because I took some horses," the man told him. "My name's Arpid. What's yours?"

"Mathayus. How can we get away from here?"

"No problem. I wasn't asleep when they put me in here. Watch those guards."

Mathayus turned his eyes to the guards. His sword, knives, and arrows were on the ground next to them. One guard looked carefully at the sword. The other man turned his back for a minute.

Mathayus looked back at his new friend—but Arpid wasn't there!

The guards looked too and ran to Mathayus.

"Where is he?" they shouted.

Suddenly, Arpid was behind them, and he killed them.

"Get me out of here," Mathayus shouted, "or I will kill you!"

"That's not very nice. What will you give me?"

Mathayus looked at him angrily. The words came slowly: "*Please* will you . . . help me? I won't kill you."

"Really?"

"Yes, really."

When Mathayus was free, he found his knives and arrows.

"I'll come with you," Arpid said. "You can kill people and I'll take their money. OK?"

Mathayus called to Hanna, and the camel walked slowly out of the desert. Then Mathayus rode away.

"Stop!" Arpid shouted. "You can't go without me. You wanted to kill that woman, the sorcerer, but you couldn't. And now you have to do it. But where is she? You don't know, but *I* know."

Mathayus stopped and waited for him.

Chapter 5   "You will be my wife."

In the center of the city of Gomorrah stood Memnon's palace.
Inside, Cassandra moved her fingers across a map.

"What can my sorcerer tell me today?" asked Memnon. He
was with Thorak and Takmet.

"The people of Ur are very unhappy about their king," she
answered, and Takmet smiled. "They are leaving their homes."

"And the Nubian—Balthazar?" Memnon asked.

"I cannot see Balthazar and his people," she said slowly.

Memnon turned to Thorak and Takmet.

"Tell the fighters about Ur," he said "They will leave
tomorrow." The two men left, and Memnon turned back to
Cassandra. "I am the Teacher of Men," he said. "The world will
be a better place. That is the future. You saw it. When it happens,
you will be my wife. You will be with me in my bed."

Cassandra's smile was cold.

Cassandra moved her fingers across a map.

"In your bed I will be a woman, not a sorcerer," she told him. "I will not know the future."

"But when I am king of the world, there will be no more fighting. Then you can be a woman for me."

He took her arm.

Cassandra moved away. Suddenly, she saw a picture in her head. She saw Mathayus in the desert. So he wasn't dead? She said nothing to Memnon.

"Cassandra, you are important to me," Memnon told her. He loved her, but he couldn't tell her that.

"You are very good to me," Cassandra said, and she walked away. She hated him.

◆

Mathayus and Arpid looked down at Gomorrah. There were guards everywhere on the walls around the city.

Mathayus and Arpid looked down at Gomorrah.

Arpid looked unhappy.

"I can't help you," he said. "The guards know me. I'll make things difficult for you and . . ."

"You are coming with me," Mathayus told him. "Let's go."

"I *know* I can't help," Arpid said.

"Yes, you can," Mathayus said, and hit him hard.

Arpid fell to the ground and didn't move.

Mathayus walked to the doors of the city with his camel. Arpid was on Hanna's back.

"What do you want?" a guard asked the Akkadian.

"I have Arpid with me." He showed the little man to the guard. "He took some horses. Memnon wants him."

Another guard looked at Arpid. "I know him," he said. "They'll kill him this time."

So Mathayus walked into Gomorrah. He found some water and pushed Arpid's head into it.

Arpid woke up.

"What happened?" he asked.

"We are inside," Mathayus told him. "Thank you for your help. Now stay with my camel."

He left Arpid in a bar and walked to Memnon's palace. Some small boys followed him.

"Can you show me a way into this place?" he asked them.

"That's *not* a good idea," one child said.

The boys laughed and ran around him. Then one boy cut Mathayus's bag of rubies from his coat and ran away. Mathayus went after him, but the child threw the bag to another boy. He threw it to a different boy. Where was the bag now? In the end, Mathayus found the right child and took his bag. Then he opened the boy's mouth and took out the last ruby.

The boy laughed.

"I had to try."

Mathayus smiled.

13

"Do you want this ruby?" Mathayus asked. "Show me a way into the palace."

Chapter 6 "We will make you very happy."

Mathayus looked down at Memnon. He was with his fighting teacher. The teacher shot an arrow at Memnon. Memnon caught it in his hand. The people around them laughed.

Mathayus took out an arrow too. He was ready. Memnon couldn't see him—he couldn't catch *his* arrow.

Then two guards arrived with a prisoner. It was the boy, and he was between Mathayus and Memnon. No! Mathayus stopped and watched.

One of the guards showed the ruby to Memnon.

"Where did he find that? Kill him!" Memnon said.

The guard took out his sword—and Mathayus's arrow flew down to him. Some of the other guards quickly took Memnon away. More guards ran after Mathayus.

Mathayus ran too and found a small room. Thick smoke and strange noises came from glass bottles: *hssssss, pooof*. A man walked out of the smoke, and Mathayus stopped him with his sword. The man was small with white hair and looked friendly.

"I am Philos," the little man said. "Can I help you, sir?"

"How can I get out of here?" Mathayus asked.

Before Philos could answer, they heard people outside: "Open the door!"

The Akkadian turned, ready for a fight.

"No, no, no . . . No fighting in here," Philos said. "Come this way."

When Philos opened the door to Thorak and his guards, Mathayus was not in the room. Thorak looked around it. Then he looked at the glass bottles.

The Akkadian turned, ready for a fight.

"Why does Memnon like your work?" he said. "I do not understand it. One day the Teacher of Men will be bored with you. Then I will watch you die."

Philos's face was white.

"Good day to you too, sir."

Thorak and the guards left, and Mathayus came out from under a table.

"Thank you," he said.

The little man looked at him sadly.

"These are difficult times," he said. "Memnon is killing a lot of people. Who are our friends when we have to hate everybody?"

He started to put his things quickly into a large bag.

Mathayus ran through the palace and opened a door. The room was full of beautiful women.

"A man!" one of the women cried.

Mathayus ran through the palace and opened a door.

Mathayus put his hand over her pretty mouth.

"Quiet!" he said. Then he turned to the other women. "Who are you?" he asked.

"Memnon's women, of course," one girl told him quietly. "But he doesn't come here often. He's always fighting. We get bored."

"Stay with us," another woman said. "We will make you very happy."

They all moved nearer him.

Suddenly, they had his sword, his knives, and his arrows, and they shouted for help. Thorak and six of his men ran into the room.

"It is the Akkadian! He lives . . . Kill him!" Thorak shouted.

Mathayus ran past them and into another room. It was a

beautiful room, a woman's room. In the center of it there was a large pool, with flowers on top of the water. Cassandra sat in the pool. Her eyes were large.

For a minute she couldn't speak. Then she climbed out of the pool and said, "Are you going to kill me, Akkadian? Or are you going to stand and look?"

But the guards were at the door. Mathayus jumped into the pool and pulled Cassandra under the water with him. When the guards came in, they couldn't see anybody. Memnon followed them.

Under the water, at the bottom of the pool, Mathayus opened a small metal door and the water began to run out.

Memnon could see them now.

"Kill him!" he cried.

But the water carried Mathayus and Cassandra out of the pool and down, down, down.

Chapter 7   "Memnon wants his sorcerer."

Arpid sat in the street and drank. He could hear a noise from Memnon's guards.

"They have the Akkadian now," he thought.

He stood up and left.

In the next street, some women washed their clothes in a pool. One woman's child found some money on the road.

"What can I do with this?" the small boy thought.

He looked at the water and threw the money into it.

A beautiful woman came up from the bottom of the pool! An Akkadian followed her. They had no clothes! The mother put her hand over her child's eyes and pulled him away. Other people came and watched.

"Cassandra, you are going to come with me now," Mathayus

"Cassandra, you are going to come with me now."

told her, and he showed her his knife. "But first, some clothes . . ."

He bought some clothes from the women around the pool, and then they left Gomorrah.

Arpid was outside the city too. He wanted to sell Hanna, and to buy a nice horse. But Hanna made loud, angry noises and nobody wanted to buy her.

A long way away, the Akkadian heard his camel and called to her. Hanna ran to Mathayus and pulled Arpid after her.

Arpid stood up and saw Cassandra.

"Who's your beautiful friend?" he asked.

"The sorcerer."

"This is Memnon's sorcerer?"

"That's right." Mathayus turned to Cassandra. "Get on the camel. We are going to the Place of the Dead."

"You're crazy!" Arpid said. "Nobody goes there and lives! Memnon and his fighters never go there!"

"They will go there when *she* is there," Mathayus said. "Memnon wants his sorcerer. He cannot win without her."

◆

Thorak and Takmet stood in front of the Teacher of Men. There was a scorpion on the table in front of him.

"Take your best men," Memnon told Thorak. "Find him and kill him. Then bring Cassandra to me." Memnon cut the scorpion with his knife and killed it. Then he took an arrow and pushed one end into the scorpion's poison. "When you see the Akkadian," he said, "give him this for me."

An hour later, Thorak and his strongest fighters rode out of the city into the desert.

◆

Mathayus, Cassandra, Arpid, and Hanna arrived at the Place of the Dead. It was hot, very hot, and there were dead men

Mathayus, Cassandra, Arpid, and Hanna arrived at the Place of the Dead.

everywhere on the ground. When night came, they stopped. They slept on the sand.

Cassandra woke up and looked around her. She stood up slowly—and then ran. But something caught her foot and she fell. Mathayus stood over her.

"Where are you going?" he asked. "Are you looking for Memnon, your lover?"

Cassandra fought him, but he pushed her down again.

"He is *not* my lover," she told him. "I have no lover. When I was eleven, Memnon heard about me. I was different from other children. He came to my home and gave me some tests. Then his guards killed my family and he took me away."

Mathayus looked at her sadly.

"I am sorry," he said. "You are not my prisoner now. You can run away and I will not stop you."

The Akkadian slept again.

Cassandra sat next to him and thought. Who was this man? *What* was he? She was a sorcerer, but she couldn't see his future.

Chapter 8   "One man on a camel . . ."

Mathayus sat on his white camel with Cassandra and looked out over the desert.

"Thorak . . ." he said.

Then he turned around. The sky was dark behind him. He smiled.

Arpid, on foot, looked up.

"How many men does he have? Can you see?"

"Only about twelve."

"Oh, only twelve? And there are three of us. One fighter, one woman, and me . . . What are we going to do now?"

"Stay here," Mathayus said.

He helped Cassandra down from the camel and rode away.

"There!" one of Thorak's men called to Thorak. "One man on a camel and he's coming this way. Is he crazy? There are thirteen of us!"

But there was a strong wind behind Mathayus, and sand flew around him and over him. Thorak's men pulled out their swords, but they couldn't see him. Then the wind hit them. Men and horses fell under the wall of sand.

Mathayus jumped down and killed two fighters, then three more. Thorak, on his horse, saw him and rode after him. But the Akkadian knew and turned. They fought, and Mathayus won the fight. But before Thorak died, he pushed Memnon's arrow, and its poison, into Mathayus's leg.

When the wind moved away, the desert was quiet again. Arpid stood up and looked around. Then he remembered the woman and helped her.

Thorak's men pulled out their swords . . .

"The Akkadian!" she said. "We have to look for him."

"Of course," Arpid answered. He felt sad. Sad? He never felt sad about another man.

Some horses came to them. Their riders were dead. Then—was that Hanna?

Arpid ran to the camel.

"Where is he?" he asked.

The camel made a noise and turned her head. And, very slowly, a man stood up. Sand fell from him.

"Are you all right?" Mathayus asked Cassandra.

"I'm fine, thanks," Arpid said. Why wasn't the Akkadian interested in *him*?

Then Mathayus took the arrow in his hands and pulled it from his leg. He fell to the ground again.

Chapter 9   "The poison will always be in him."

Memnon and his best fighters stood around a table and looked at maps. Memnon talked about the fight for Ur.

He looked up when a man came in. In the man's arms were Thorak's clothes. The fighters stopped talking.

"Is something wrong?" one man, Toran, asked.

Memnon smiled. "No," he said. "But we will end this meeting now."

The fighters walked to the door, but Toran turned again.

"Why," he asked, " is the sorcerer not here today?"

"She is sick," Memnon answered angrily.

Only Takmet knew about Cassandra. "I told them nothing," he said, after the other men left.

"Why are you here and not Thorak?" said Memnon coldly. "Go! Leave me."

◆

"I told them nothing," Takmet said.

That night, Mathayus was very sick. Arpid built a fire, and Cassandra cleaned the Akkadian's leg.

"Can you help him, sorcerer?" Arpid asked quietly.

"Maybe—but the poison is very strong," she answered. "It comes from a scorpion. But that can also be a good thing because the poison will always be in him."

"That's a good thing?"

"Yes, he will be strong and nobody can poison him again. But will he live?" She sat and thought. Then she spoke again. "He will not die."

She put one hand on Mathayus's head and the other hand on his leg. She closed her eyes and her face shone with light. Arpid watched and waited.

In the morning, Mathayus woke up and opened his eyes.

"*She* did it!" Arpid told him. "I could feel it. I could *see* it."

Cassandra felt Mathayus's eyes on her and opened her eyes too. They smiled happily.

"Let's go," the Akkadian said quickly.

He climbed onto Hanna, and Cassandra and Arpid rode two of Thorak's horses.

An hour later, they heard a loud noise: *BANG!* A small man ran to them across the desert.

"I did it!" he said. "My explosives work!"

It was Philos, and he was black from head to foot. "Do you have any water?" he asked.

They had no water, but they followed some birds to a beautiful pool. They drank and drank.

Suddenly, arrows flew over their heads and they looked around. These weren't Memnon's men. Who were they?

It was Philos . . .

24

Chapter 10 "*I* make my future."

Guards took the prisoners—Mathayus, Cassandra, Arpid, and Philos—to an open place in the mountains, a world of tents and wood. Men, women, and children came and looked at the strangers. Cassandra was more beautiful than their women. The Akkadian was bigger and stronger than their fighters.

But then a large man came out of a tent—Balthazar! The Nubian stopped when he saw Mathayus.

"Akkadian!" he said. "This is nice. When we met in Pheron's country, you wanted to kill me. Now I can kill you." Mathayus said nothing. "I know that you did not finish your job. They tell me that the sorcerer lives. And your brothers are dead. Why didn't you die too?"

"Give me a sword and I will show you," Mathayus answered.

"You are a problem now. This is our place, and you know about it."

"We won't tell anybody," Arpid said quickly.

Philos spoke too. "We are sorry, sir. We didn't know about your home here. We will leave now."

"That is not possible," Balthazar said. He turned to the guards. "Take the woman and the two men away."

"Tell your men," Mathayus said. "Nobody puts a hand on the woman."

Cassandra looked at him. There was something in his eyes. Did this man love her?

Balthazar pulled out a sword. Mathayus ran to a guard and took a sword from him. Then the two big men fought.

It was a long fight, but the Akkadian won. Everybody waited. Was it the end for the Nubian?

But the Akkadian spoke.

"We are brothers, Balthazar. We want the same thing."

Mathaus ran to a guard and took a sword from him.

"Memnon will follow you here. He will kill my people. He has to have *her*—his sorcerer."

Balthazar looked at Cassandra. He knew.

"Yes," Mathayus said. "Memnon will find you. But I will stop him."

"You—one man—will stop Memnon and his fighters?"

"Yes," Mathayus said, and he moved away from Balthazar.

Balthazar thought about this.

"You can stay one night," he said. "After that, we will never meet again."

That night, the sound of music came from the fires outside the tents. Arpid and Philos ate happily and made friends. But Cassandra was very quiet. She read the pictures in her head:

Memnon stood in Gomorrah, outside his palace, and looked up at the sky. Mathayus stood behind him with his sword in his hand. A guard stood behind Mathayus. The guard saw Mathayus and took out an arrow. The arrow flew into Mathayus's back . . .

"Is there a problem?" Mathayus asked her.

"Memnon knows that I am here," she said. "His fighters will come tomorrow night."

"Then Memnon will die. I will kill him."

"No!" Cassandra cried. "I saw it. You cannot kill Memnon. You will die!"

The Akkadian smiled.

"Listen," he said. "*I* make my future."

Cassandra looked at him. How could he say that? How could he think that? Was he right? Could one man change the future?

Then the Akkadian pulled her to him and she fell into his arms.

Later that night, Mathayus slept and Cassandra watched him. She felt different now—she was not only a sorcerer, but also a woman.

She walked away and listened to the sounds in her head. Then she smiled. She knew the answer.

Cassandra climbed onto Hanna and rode the white camel out of the trees, into the desert. She was on her way to Gomorrah.

Chapter 11   "This is not your fight. It is ours."

Balthazar woke up when he heard a sound outside. He looked out and saw Arpid, Philos, and Mathayus around a fire.

"What are you planning now, Akkadian?" he asked. "And where is the sorcerer?"

Suddenly, dark, beautiful Isis stood next to him.

"She is on her way to Gomorrah," she told Balthazar.

Balthazar laughed.

"To Memnon's bed?"

Mathayus shouted angrily, "She is not his woman, and she never will be his woman."

"She is *your* woman, Akkadian? So why did she go to Gomorrah?"

"She saw Memnon and his fighters here, in this place. He wanted her—so she went back to him."

"She did this for us?"

"Yes," Mathayus said. "And now I am going after her, before he . . ."

He climbed onto a horse and rode away.

When he came out of the mountains, he saw a man in front of him. He stopped.

"I and my men will come with you, Akkadian," Balthazar said. "This is not your fight. It is ours."

Isis walked out from behind a rock.

"I and my women will come too," she said.

♦

Night fell over Gomorrah. Inside the palace, Memnon's best

Cassandra rode the white camel out of the trees, into the desert.

fighters enjoyed a party. Only Memnon was unhappy. Where was Cassandra? Was she a prisoner? Or did she *want* to be with the Akkadian?

He stood up.

"Tonight," he told his visitors, "at midnight, my time will come. You will see a scorpion in the sky, and I will be the Scorpion King. The world will be mine. All mine."

The room was quiet, then Toran stood up.

"That's wonderful," he said, "but we have a problem. Our men are talking."

"And what are they talking about?" Memnon asked.

"They are saying that the sorcerer is not with you now. They are afraid."

"But she *is* with me," Memnon answered.

"I am sorry," Toran said, "but they want to see her . . ."

He saw Memnon's face and stopped. These were dangerous words.

Memnon thought for a minute.

"I am telling you . . ." he began.

"I am late. I am very sorry." A woman stood in the doorway. It was Cassandra! She walked to Memnon, and then turned to his visitors. "I was not well, but now I am better. And I know that we are going to win our fight."

"I am sorry too," Toran said to Memnon.

"I understand," said Memnon—and he pushed his knife into Toran. "I cannot use weak men," he told the other fighters. "And now, sleep well. Tomorrow, we will fight!" He turned to Cassandra and said quietly, "Wait for me in my rooms."

Cassandra left, and Memnon watched her with cold eyes.

◆

Outside the city walls, the guards stopped Arpid and Philos. They were with six women.

Memnon watched her with cold eyes.

"We're taking them to Takmet, for tonight's party," Arpid said.

The women—Isis's fighters—laughed and talked with the guards.

On the walls there were more guards. They died quickly and quietly after Mathayus arrived behind them.

Down on the ground, one "woman" showed her face to a guard. It was Balthazar, and he killed the man. Isis's women killed the other guards.

Mathayus looked around him. Everything was quiet. He called to his camel. Hanna ran to him from the center of the city. Mathayus climbed down to his friends and put his arms around the white camel.

"Does everybody understand our plan?" he asked.

"Yes," they answered.

Arpid's eyes were wet.

"What's wrong?" Mathayus asked.

Arpid looked at the ground.

"This is my first important job," he said. "Thank you. I'll do it well."

"I know you will."

Balthazar said, "Akkadian!" Mathayus turned. "Be careful!"

Mathayus smiled—and then he rode into the city. His friends followed.

Chapter 12   "I am here for the woman."

Memnon looked at his sorcerer. His eyes weren't friendly.

"Why didn't the Akkadian kill you?" he asked.

"He wanted *you*," Cassandra answered. "He took me because he wanted you to follow us."

"Did you see Thorak?"

Memnon looked at his sorcerer. His eyes weren't friendly.

"I was there when he died. I could not do anything. Then later, I ran away."

For a long time Memnon said nothing. Then he asked, "Did the Akkadian put his hands on you?"

"No, Memnon."

He took her to a chair.

"Wait here, my dear."

She sat and waited. The night was warm, but she felt very cold.

◆

In the center of the city, Philos showed Isis and her fighter women a metal door in the street.

A guard called to them, but Isis killed him quickly. More guards ran and fought the women. But the women won easily and without a sound.

33

With his strong hands, Balthazar opened the metal door.

"Let's go," Arpid said to Philos.

The two little men carried Philos's bags of explosives inside and took them down under the palace.

♦

Memnon sat and watched his sorcerer.

"I can feel a change in you," he said.

"I am not different from before," she said.

"So you can really see the future? A great future for me?"

"Of course."

But through the window, on the outside wall, Cassandra could see Mathayus.

The Akkadian jumped into the room and onto Memnon.

"I am here for the woman," he shouted. "And for your head."

The two men took out their swords and fought.

Cassandra closed the doors. She didn't want Memnon's fighters to come in. Then she took a sword from the wall and watched Memnon carefully.

Chapter 13   "Go after her—friend."

Isis and her fighters waited outside the palace. Suddenly, there were guards everywhere.

"Oh, no!" Isis said.

Balthazar ran to the guards.

"Which of you wants to die first?" he asked.

He killed them, and then he walked inside.

♦

Arpid and Philos moved quickly. When they were under Memnon's rooms, they opened the bags. They put a long line of black explosive across the floor from the bags. Then they started a small fire at the end of the line.

But when they ran away from the fire, Arpid's foot broke the line of explosive. Behind them, the fire slowly died.

The two little men waited outside for ten minutes.

"Nothing's happening," Philos said unhappily. "We have to go back."

"You're crazy," Arpid told him. "I don't want to die."

But Philos ran into Memnon's palace, this time through the doors. Arpid watched and then followed him.

They went down below the building and found the explosives. They started another fire and ran away again. But Arpid ran into a wall and fell to the ground.

Philos stopped.

"Why did I bring him with me?" he thought. "The camel is better than he is."

He carried Arpid out of the palace.

◆

Cassandra couldn't get behind Memnon with her sword, but Mathayus fought well.

Loud noises came from the doors, and then Balthazar broke through them. Four guards ran after him, but he killed them. More guards arrived and he killed them too. Memnon was suddenly afraid. How many fighters did the Akkadian have?

Guard after guard came through the door and Balthazar's arms were tired now. Then a guard's sword cut the Nubian's leg.

"Mathayus!" cried Cassandra. "You have to help Balthazar!"

The Akkadian pushed Memnon away. He ran to Balthazar and killed some guards. Then Balthazar was ready for another fight.

Memnon's eyes were on Cassandra. He ran at her, and her sword flew away. Then he took her in his arms and ran from the room.

Memnon was suddenly afraid.

"Are you all right, my friend?" Mathayus asked Balthazar.
The Nubian smiled.

"Go after her—friend. I'll stay with the guards."
Mathayus ran through the palace.

Chapter 14 "The Scorpion King!"

Philos pushed Arpid through the door into the street. Isis helped
him.

"Don't ask!" Philos said to her.

"But this time the explosives will work?"

"Yes—but I don't know when."

◆

Memnon put Cassandra down outside.

"You betrayed me!" he said. "And did you really see my great
future?"

"I saw it," she said. "And I wanted to stop it!"

Memnon looked up. Then he took her arm and pulled her
behind him.

"It is almost midnight. It is my time now," he told her.

Cassandra fought him, but he was stronger. Then a man ran
out from the palace and jumped onto Memnon. It was the
Akkadian.

◆

There were dead men everywhere on the floor around Balthazar.
He stood for a minute and listened. It was quiet. No—was that
the sound of a horse? *Inside* the building?

Takmet rode in. What could Balthazar do? But the Nubian
was stronger. He pulled Takmet off his horse and threw him at a
wall.

Takmet looked up at him.

"End it now," he said.

Balthazar showed him his large hand.

"This is for your father," he said.

He hit Takmet very hard between the eyes.

◆

Mathayus and Memnon fought, and Cassandra could do nothing. She cried when Memnon almost pushed the Akkadian from a high wall. But Mathayus jumped down. Then Memnon hit him and he fell.

Suddenly, Memnon's eyes weren't on Mathayus. He looked up at the sky. Was that a scorpion, high above them?

Cassandra thought quickly. She thought about the earlier pictures in her head. She knew the future. A man with an arrow—but where? From which door? She looked around and she saw the door.

Mathayus was on his feet and ready again.

"*Mathayus!*"

He turned to Cassandra and saw, behind her, the man with the arrow. He understood. In her head, this was the end for him. She wanted to change his future, so *she* had to die.

He ran to her quickly and turned his back to the arrow. It hit him.

"No!" Cassandra cried.

When Mathayus fell, Memnon smiled. Then he looked up again at the sky.

Cassandra took the guard's sword and killed the man. Mathayus started to move very slowly across the ground.

"I am Memnon—king of the world," the Teacher of Men called to the sky. "I am not a man now. Nobody can kill me."

Mathayus's arrow hit him—and, below them, the fire arrived at Philos's explosives.

BANG! Men and buildings fell. Memnon, with the arrow inside him, went over the wall, down into the city street.

Arpid, Philos, Isis, and her fighters watched him fall. Then they looked up and saw Mathayus. Cassandra moved next to him—and then Balthazar, too, arrived at the top of the wall.

In the sky, the scorpion shone over Mathayus.

"The Scorpion King!" Philos said.

Arpid smiled.

"And my friend!"

Chapter 15   "What will the future bring us?"

The next morning, the streets of Gomorrah were full of smoke. Mathayus, the new king, walked with Cassandra through the city. The people watched and smiled.

At the doors of the city, the Akkadian and the sorcerer said goodbye to Balthazar and Isis.

"Stay, my friend," Mathayus said to the big Nubian. "There is work here."

Balthazar smiled.

"I have to go to my people now," he said. "You have your white camel and your two little men. They will help you. But you are a king now, not a killer. Don't forget your past—or your people."

"My people are dead," the Akkadian said.

The Nubian looked at Cassandra.

"But there will be children."

Mathayus laughed.

"There will always be a place here for you—and for you," he told Isis.

Balthazar's smile left his face.

"Be good, Scorpion King," he said. "Nubian eyes will watch you."

Then he and Isis, with her fighters, rode away into the desert.
The Scorpion King turned to the woman next to him.

"And what will the future bring us, my sorcerer?"

Cassandra thought about his question.

"Good times," she answered.

Mathayus looked across the desert and saw a black sky.

"And problems," he said.

"Yes, there will be problems. But those are new stories."

"*We* will make our future," he told her, and he took her in his arms.

Cassandra saw pictures in her head, but she said nothing. Mathayus was a king now. The future really was another story.

"And what will the future bring us, my sorcerer?"

ACTIVITIES

Chapters 1–5

Before you read

1 Answer these questions. Find the words in *italics* in your dictionary.
   They are all in the story.
   a Does a *king* or a *sorcerer* usually live in a *palace*?
   b Do you find a lot of trees or *rocks* and *sand* in a *desert*?
   c Can you *ride* a *camel* or a *ruby*?
   d Do you kill people or cook for them with *arrows* and a *sword*?
   e Does a *guard* watch a *prisoner* or a small child?
   f Does a *tent* usually have a *chimney* or not?
   g After somebody *betrays* you, are they your friend or not?

2 Discuss possible answers to these questions about the story. Use
   the words in *italics* above.
   a Where does the story happen?
   b Who are some of the people in the story?
   c Where do they live?
   d What do they do in the story?

After you read

3 Who are they? Find the right names below.
   a the Akkadians
   b the Teacher of Men
   c the King of Ur and his son
   d the Nubians
   e the dirty white camel
   f the sorcerer

   Balthazar and Isis   Pheron and Takmet   Hanna
   Mathayus, Jesup, and Rama   Memnon   Cassandra

4 Answer these questions about Arpid.
   a Why is he a prisoner?
   b Why does he want to help Mathayus?
   c Why does Mathayus hit him?

41

Chapters 6–10

Before you read

5 Discuss these questions. Mathayus wants to go into Memnon's palace. Why? What does he want to do there? Will it be easy? Will it be dangerous? Why (not)?

6 Find these words in your dictionary. Which of these things are always dangerous?

explosive   metal   poison   scorpion

After you read

7 Who says these words? Who to? Who or what are they talking about?

a "Where did he find that? Kill him!"

b "Nobody goes there and lives."

c "Is he crazy? There are thirteen of us."

d The poison will always be in him."

e I know that you did not finish your job."

8 Work with another student. Have this conversation.

Student A: You are Arpid. You are standing outside the city of Gomorrah. You are trying to sell Hanna.

Student B: You want to buy a fast, cheap, friendly camel.

Chapters 11–15

Before you read

9 What does Cassandra know now about Mathayus's future? What do you think she is going to do in Gomorrah?

After you read

10 Who lives? Who dies?

Arpid   Balthazar   Cassandra   Isis   Mathayus   Memnon
Philos   Takmet   Toran

11 Work with another student. Have this conversation.

Student A: You are Cassandra. You can see a very difficult and dangerous future for Mathayus. What is it? Do you tell him about it or not?

Student B: You are Cassandra's friend. Listen to her and ask questions. What do you think?

42

Writing

12 Write the story of *The Scorpion King*. Don't write more than 100 words.

13 Which person in the story did you like best? Why? Write about that person.

14 You live in Gomorrah. Write a letter to a friend in another city. Write about Memnon, your old king, and Mathayus, your new king. How is life different for you now?

15 Write a conversation between Balthazar and Isis on their way to their Nubian people, at the end of the story.

MOST POPULAR
PENGUIN READERS

AT LEVEL 2

Anne of Green Gables

Apollo 13

Babe - The Sheep-Pig

A Christmas Carol

E.T. The Extra-Terrestrial

Jumanji

Men in Black

Mr Bean

The Mummy

The Secret Garden

Treasure Island

White Fang